HOW TO BE A WHOLESOME VEGETARIAN:

A Superb Manual for Turning Vegetarian and Staying Healthy

By

KENNETH J. BRATSON

LEGAL NOTICE

subject Matter herein. Any perceived slights of specific persons, peoples, or organizations are unintentional.

In practical advice books, like anything else in life, there are no guarantees of income made. Readers are cautioned to reply on their own judgment about their individual circumstances to act accordingly.

This book is not intended for use as a source of legal, business, accounting or financial advice. All readers are advised to seek services of competent professionals in legal, business, accounting and finance fields.

You are encouraged to print this book for easy reading.

TABLE OF CONTENTS

- It is true that cooking vegetarian meals is among the simplest skills to learn. Vegetarian food is incredibly intriguing and simple to prepare, even for people who are afraid of boiling water or cooking food.

CHAPTER 6: VEGGIE LOW CARB

- To keep healthy, human bodies require a variety of nutrients. Vegetarianism is healthy, but you must carefully balance your intake of vitamins and nutrients. The carbohydrate balance is the only thing that needs to cross your attention.

CHAPTER 7: VEGETARIAN AND NON-VEGETARIAN

- Given that the eating habits are unique and evident, the distinction between vegetarianism and non-vegetarianism is well acknowledged

INTRODUCTION

Change is never easy to embrace, and switching to a vegetarian diet is more difficult than you might think.

Therefore, prior to adjusting to a new way of life, thorough research is crucial. It may be difficult to transition to a meat-free diet from time to time. Since becoming a vegetarian entail much more than simply cutting out meat, it is preferable to be aware of the benefits and drawbacks in advance.

There are many different kinds of vegetarians, some of whom eat fish more frequently than others. On the other hand, there are people who live solely on fruits and vegetables and avoid dairy products like cheese and eggs.

It is always an individual's preference to eat vegetarian. Before avoiding cottage cheese and other nutritious foods that provide essential nourishment, one must also consider the nutritional supplements that the body would require.

To become a vegetarian completely, it is preferable to begin slowly and progress slowly. Although it's hard to believe, the body's entire system will undergo significant changes because the body won't be receiving something it is accustomed to.

It is always preferable to reduce consumption in stages rather than abruptly eliminating meat from one's regular diet, substituting fish or chicken for it, and eventually becoming a vegetarian.

Knowing the nutritional content of the foods you would eat instead of meat is the most important part of going vegetarian. Most people who don't like vegetarianism think that if they don't eat meat, their body won't get enough of the essential vitamins and minerals it needs.

Despite this, a lot of people have been able to successfully transition to a meat-free diet. These people have been able to give their bodies the nutrients it needs, making up for the lack of meat in their diet.

Numerous studies have demonstrated that eating green vegetables like broccoli, kale, and spinach, which are high in calcium, provides the necessary nutrients for health.

Nuts are also known to be a good source of protein. Such vegetarian diets can guarantee sufficient nutrition for a healthy life and a well-balanced diet.

One of the most important things you can do to make your body feel healthy is to eat vegetarian. And those who have already made the switch to a vegan diet must have realized that they feel great, have a lot of energy, and were able to lose weight without going hungry. Therefore, start considering this and move forward toward a life that you enjoy.

CHAPTER 1: GETTING STARTED AS A VEGETARIAN

Imagine the efforts a person would need to make to learn how to switch to a vegetarian diet, and it can seem unrealistic.

However, cutting off meat entirely from one's diet is not the only option. The answer to that simple question is... not really. People think that becoming a vegan needs a lot more work than just forgoing meat or hamburger.

To be fit and avoid depriving one's body of what it fundamentally needs to function perfectly in the way it was intended to, becoming a vegan involves extensive research and substantial work, as everyone who gives it a try will discover.

When switching to a vegan diet, taking it slowly is the most important thing to try. A relaxed approach won't make much of a difference if you've been eating meat regularly for a while.

Making the switch to veganism will require some determined and serious effort. Start by gradually cutting meat from your daily diet.

You can skip eating meat for a few days before switching to fish or chicken. As the body gradually adjusts to the change in diet, this procedure can eventually assist you in stopping meat permanently.

In order to ensure that their body is receiving the nutrients it needs to be well-built and efficient, a person must understand how to adopt a lacta-vegetarian diet and do a brief investigation into the nutrients that are present in various vegetables. It is important to remember that vitamins like B and C, as well as minerals like iron and zinc, are necessary for human health.

One would want to know the nutritional content of the food they are ingesting because calcium and protein are also essential parts of a balanced diet. It is crucial to make sure the body receives all the important vitamins and nutrients it needs to function properly.

People who are cutting out meat from their diets need to make sure they are getting enough protein into their bodies. Protein is essential to human health, thus those learning how to become vegans will want to find other sources of protein so that their bodies can function as they were meant to.

Vegetarian Diet – Healthy

Vegan diets are recognized to be exceptionally wholesome and robust, but eating a decent diet when one is a vegetarian frequently gets little extra attention. When someone excludes red meat and animal protein from their diet, they are eliminating a major source of protein that their body needs. It follows that including foods in one's diet that are nutrient-rich and often present in animal products is necessary for a vegan to have a healthy diet.

People can easily obtain the vitamins and nutrients they require from vegetarian sources by experimenting with a diet consisting of fruits, vegetables, and whole grains, ensuring that their vegetarian lifestyle is balanced and healthy.

One can get the necessary protein content they need for growth by eating foods like eggs, almonds, soy products, and legumes. It's also important to remember that vegans require a similar amount of other nutrients, including the vitamins D and B12, the minerals calcium and iron, and the vitamin D.

However, it is true that cutting out meat and replacing it with a diet high in vegetables, fruits, and whole grains is healthful. However, vegetarians must also worry about other important elements, such as getting the correct ratio of vitamins and minerals in their diet.

Many people can regularly take a vitamin supplement, however since many of these products contain animal products, many ardent vegetarians avoid taking them. Since iron, niacin, and vitamins B and C are all key components of a healthy lacto-vegetarian diet, it is imperative that one seek for a diet high in these nutrients.

If someone chooses to become a vegan, they don't have to sacrifice their health. It is difficult to consume a healthy vegetarian diet. It is strictly necessary to set aside leisure time to research and locate dietary items that contain the nutrients that the body needs the most. You may need to spend a lot of time reading numerous books, publications, and even the internet for this.

When people stop eating, they can replace meat with a variety of foods in their diet. For instance, one can choose soy milk as a substitute to cow's milk, which would help the body get the calcium it needs. Vegetarianism can be transformed into a nutritious diet by adding nuts and grains to it. Furthermore, grains and nuts are a great source of proteins, which support the growth of strong bones.

CHAPTER 2: VEGETARIAN DIET FOR LOSING WEIGHT

Many people decide to become vegetarians because they must follow a diet in order to lose weight yet detest the thought of starving themselves

Because you are eliminating all red meat from your diet, which can include a lot of fat that is stored in your body's cells and contributes to weight gain, going vegetarian can help you lose weight in a variety of other ways as well. A vegetarian consumes a lot of healthful foods like fruits, vegetables, fish, and shellfish, all of which can help you lose weight.

You should really think about switching to a vegetarian lifestyle because dieting is challenging when you want to lose weight. Since vegetables are healthy and naturally low in calories, you won't have to worry about gaining weight while eating them.

Fruits are nutritious for you, but because the body likes to retain water, they are also quite high in water content and can cause you to weigh extra.

A solid, well-rounded vegetarian diet designed for maximum weight loss includes a variety of tasty foods and satiating spices. You know, the way we prepare food and the ingredients we use can make it fattening.

Even if you eat a bowlful of nutritious mushrooms, cooking them in butter and heavy cream to make a soup will add calories and nullify their naturally beneficial effects.

As far as possible, avoid frying your food if you're following a vegetarian diet to lose weight. If you want to sauté any of your vegetables, use extra virgin olive oil, or EVOO as Rachel Ray calls it. This oil has fewer calories and some of the healthy fats your body requires.

Additionally, you should avoid high-fat cheeses and choose lower-fat types, as well as look at alternatives like substituting plain yogurt for sour cream.

A vegetarian diet is both a fantastic tool for losing weight and a healthy diet. We're prepared to wager that you'll keep up your vegetarian diet once you reach your weight loss objectives.

Being a vegetarian is easier than many people realize. If you cultivate the majority of your vegetables, you'll notice that you have more energy, a faster metabolism (which burns fat), and lower food costs.

Therefore, choose a vegetarian diet for optimum weight reduction and watch the pounds melt off without constantly feeling hungry.

CHAPTER 3: PRACTICING VEGETARIANISM

A fantastic path to health is being a vegetarian. It ultimately promotes a lot healthier lifestyle in addition to aiding in the retrieval of in-store metabolism

We frequently encounter neighbors who need to change their diets because they have a condition that may have been brought on by an unhealthy diet. Being a vegetarian could aid someone in maintaining a careful eye on their health because those who eat meat are more likely to develop diabetes and high cholesterol.

Vegetarians are typically thought to consume a lot of green salad, but this perception is partly mistaken because, from a larger viewpoint, the categorization is very different from what is typically thought.

The following are a handful of the groups that were mentioned:

• Lacto-ovo-vegetarians – Individuals who favor eating both dairy and eggs. The vegetarian diet that is most frequently chosen by vegetarians.

• Lacto-vegetarians – People who fall into this category eat dairy products but no eggs.

• Vegans are those who don't eat any dairy products, eggs, or other animal products.

• Fruitarians are classified as vegans when they consume the fewest processed foods possible while still maintaining an optimal level of nutrition. It primarily consists of uncooked fruits, grains, and nuts. Fruitarians only consume food that can be picked without harming the plant, according to their philosophy.

• Macrobiotic – People who follow this diet do so for moral and intellectual reasons. With an understanding of the positive and negative energy that food contains, it is taken into account. The yin is its positive quality, whereas the yang is its adverse quality. This eating pattern seeks to keep up a healthy diet. This diet becomes more specialized after ten levels.

Even though vegetarians make up the majority of the population, eliminating all animal products and, in certain extreme circumstances, even fruits and vegetables, results in a diet that solely contains brown rice.

Everyone has different motivations for being a vegetarian. For example, some people do it because they don't want to harm animals, while others do it because they believe it to be a healthier lifestyle choice. Whatever the cause, vegetarians live far healthier lives than non-vegetarians, as demonstrated by medical research.

Vegetarians have lower odds of developing diabetes, cholesterol buildup, and even some types of cancer. The risk of consuming toxic chemicals—about which scientists have demonstrated to cause major damage to the appropriate functioning of the body and neurological system—is eliminated when food is grown organically with minimal usage of pesticides.

Go ahead and take the first step toward a much healthier life if this has in any way convinced you to pursue a vegetarian lifestyle. It might be quite demanding and challenging at first, but over time, it would result in significant improvements that would make people lot safer and healthier.

CHAPTER 4: DIETARY SUPPLEMENTS FOR ATHLETES

Let's imagine that despite being a vegan and being quite active in sports, you are concerned about eating the correct foods.

Not to worry. You may maintain a vegetarian lifestyle and engage in physical activity while getting all the nourishment you require. Just because you don't want to eat meat doesn't mean you have to change your diet.

In fact, you could discover that a vegetarian diet makes it quite easy for you to engage in physical activity because the nutrients in grains, vegetables, and other plant foods really offer you greater energy.

The first thing you should keep in mind is that you must eat before exercising so that your body can start processing the food and provide you with the nutrition you need to survive a rigorous workout and have the energy to engage in the sports you enjoy.

This means that vegetarians must consume a lot of carbs prior to engaging in physical activity so that the nutrients found in those foods can do its job.

In order to replace the nutrition that is naturally lost through sweat during your workout, you should have a healthy vegetarian meal right after you finish engaging in your sport.

However, you should try to limit your intake of carbohydrates at this meal because they are rapidly converted to fat, which would undo all the advantages you have just given yourself.

If you are a lacto-vegetarian who is actively interested in sports, we advise that you consume a lot of nuts, grains, and fruits that are high in carbs and can replenish your body's water supply, which will be lost through sweat during your athletic workouts.

Since exercise is so crucial to staying in shape, vegetarian athletes frequently worry about their diet. All they actually need to keep in mind is that certain vitamins and minerals are necessary for the body to operate properly. When it comes to it, research is important.

In order to prevent their nutrition from suffering, ask some of your vegetarian friends what they do prior to participating in sports. Look online for tips on how to maximize the nutrition in your vegetarian diet before engaging in physical activity.

If you're a vegetarian who does a lot of sports and you're concerned about nutrition, read books and see your doctor along the way. You can never have too much information, so look for what's available to you and then pay attention. In the end, it will all be worthwhile!

CHAPTER 5: MAKING VEGETARIAN FOOD ACCESSIBLE TO ALL

It is true that cooking vegetarian meals is among the simplest skills to learn. Vegetarian food is incredibly intriguing and simple to prepare, even for people who are afraid of boiling water or cooking food.

Everyone can prepare vegetarian meals. It is not only highly nutritious but also simple for anyone to prepare vegetarian meals.

The best-selling book "Vegetarian Cooking for Everyone" was just released by America's top chef, Deborah Madison. You shouldn't consider it to be another cookbook for vegetarians. It includes 800 scrumptious recipes as well as crucial information on the elements and techniques of cooking.

The book teaches innovative techniques for making well-known foods like guacamole as well as obscure ones like green lentils with roasted beets and preserved lemons and cashew curry. The book is freely accessible everywhere and costs only $26.40 on Amazon.com.

The 124-page chapter on veggies, titled "The Heart of Matter," can be used as a reference for any vegetarian culinary abilities, according to an Amazon review. It might have been used as a guide or as assistance when purchasing veggies. Madison offers equally creative recipes and advice for various types of foods, including grains, soy, dairy products, and sweets.

It has proven to be an excellent resource and has made learning enjoyable for all of its readers. One reviewer even admitted that the author's writing about recipes for the typical kitchen is what draws readers of all ages. It's not like those chef books where the reader or student finds it challenging to prepare the recipes.

Everyone should read "Vegetarian Cooking for Everyone." Even a mediocre cook who reads from it can plan or cook good meals. A novice or new learner who can successfully create tasty vegetarian meals will find this to be of great assistance as it will boost his confidence. It has been determined that "Vegetarian Cooking for Everyone" is a thorough book that is interesting to everyone, including those who want to use it as a resource for regular cooking. Every meal is covered, including appetizers, sizzlers, snacks, breakfast, lunch, and supper. It's easy to find the ingredients in one's cupboard and refrigerator, and using them to make something delicious is quite satisfying and enjoyable.

Cooking Upscale Vegetarian Food

There are a ton of chances for vegans who enjoy preparing upscale foods to explore and discover. You can prepare a large variety of epicurean vegan foods in a variety of settings and circumstances; you simply need to look for opportunities.

Unfortunately, due to space restrictions, we are unable to list every cookbook available in this brief post. However, there are a few suggestions I can make for great vegetarian food preparation.

First, let's define an epicurean meal. Now, the issue of feasibility arises. A gourmet lunch is actually a special meal without meat or pasta that involves combining intriguing and uncommon ingredients to create dishes that are not only delicious but also visually stunning.

Gourmet can be defined in a variety of ways, but making gourmet vegan food requires a certain level of skill. It demands a lot of flavor and the capacity to transform ordinary components into works of beauty.

So what information is required to prepare a gourmet vegetarian meal? If they have been a lacto-vegetarian for a while, they may want to think about what they enjoy eating and how to add creativity to make it interesting and delectable in addition to scrumptious.

The greatest method for introducing vegetarian food to individuals is to think about the kinds of gourmet meals they have previously enjoyed. It is absolutely true that practically all of us have eaten vegetarian meals. It's important to always explore for methods to make a dish without the meat and keep the flavor intact.

In their neighborhood bookstore, on various websites, and online, one can find sizable and varied recipe books that are wholly devoted to gourmet vegetarian way of cooking. Search for culinary techniques that use ingredients that all find fascinating before trying the dish.

If they begin from anywhere, many people will not be able to prepare a gourmet vegetarian feast. However, if you strictly adhere to the directions, you can avoid a culinary disaster.

Being a vegan chef, preparing a gourmet dinner may be a truly adventurous and revitalizing experience. Many people think that living a vegetarian lifestyle requires confusion and curiosity. When one can simply show that they are capable of providing a vegetarian banquet that is exquisite, visually appealing, and delicious, they may just wave them over to their side of the fence.

But don't push yourself too far. A lacto-vegetarian lifestyle is not for everyone. The best thing someone can do is cook from the heart and stick to their commitment to leading a vegetarian lifestyle, which involves creating gourmet dishes that taste like they contain mutton but don't actually contain any meat.

CHAPTER 6: VEGGIE LOW CARB

To keep healthy, human bodies require a variety of nutrients. Vegetarianism is healthy, but you must carefully balance your intake of vitamins and nutrients. The carbohydrate balance is the only thing that needs to cross your attention.

Only because carbs are such a tremendous source of energy should they be consumed in moderation. An excessive amount of carbohydrates in a vegetarian diet will cause the body to produce fat. Carbs change sugar, which then turns into fat, which might be problematic if there is an excessive amount of conversion.

If you want to reduce your intake of carbohydrates, you should limit your intake of foods high in carbohydrates such rice, potatoes, and cereals. Since these foods are a good source of carbohydrates, it is also not suggested to fully exclude them from your diet. The consumption of certain food products needs to be reduced.

Additionally, flour contains carbs, including whole wheat flour. If you are serious about getting the right amount of carbohydrates, you should avoid or limit eating bread. To control the right consumption of carbohydrates, ensure that the source of your carbohydrates is acceptable. Eat whole grain bread instead of white bread to satisfy your body's need for carbohydrates.

Being a vegetarian is beneficial, but it requires a lot of sacrifices. There should be a large amount of fresh, green vegetables in the diet.

The decision to choose a vegetarian diet varies among individuals for a variety of reasons. The primary motivation is shedding additional weight. Others are really concerned about the slaughter of numerous animals. The main requirement for leading a vegetarian lifestyle is a healthy diet. An excessive intake of carbs can convert to sugar, which can progressively result in weight gain.

You must be very careful to determine the precise amount of carbohydrates available in your diet before beginning a vegetarian diet that is similarly low in carbohydrate content. Low carbohydrate intake may have an impact on your body, and most crucially, your health. Nutrition is the most crucial component of a healthy diet.

Healthy Recipes for Vegetarians

Perhaps someone who wanted to lose weight would have preferred a vegetarian way of life and needed a vegan diet low in calories to help them achieve their goals. The great news is that reducing one's intake of meat would result in low calorie consumption. The secret to making healthy vegan recipes is getting rid of the extra fat that makes meals substantial.

When making low-fat vegan dishes, folks should initially try to avoid using a lot of oil. For salads and tastings, one can still use extra virgin olive oil of the highest quality. EVOO provides some of the "beneficial fats" that our bodies require while having a lower calorie value.

While preparing vegetarian dishes with lower calorie counts, avoid eating fried items. Even if one does use the extra virgin olive oil for frying, one should avoid fried dishes as much as is practical because they typically contain more calories.

Steer clear of boiling the vegetables and instead steam them. Significant nutrients will be lost during boiling. For a change, grill some vegetables. To give them some moisture, you may also spritz on a low-calorie or light cooking spray, or even sprinkle some watery lemon juice on top.

If one must consume seafood due to their diet, boil the fish rather than frying it. It is recommended to grill the fish because it is a great way to add flavor and uniqueness to food. Spices are key components that can make a significant difference and offer a delicious and enticing low-fat vegetarian recipe.

Online resources abound for low-calorie vegetarian cooking. Cookbooks for vegetarians that contain low-fat recipes are also available. Simple substitutions like diet cheeses or plain yogurt for vinegary cream are a more efficient and practical way to create vegetarian recipes that are low in calories.

If a person is inventive, they will be astounded to learn that there are a ton of nutritious vegetarian meals available, and that they may incorporate these recipes into their diets to balance their weight loss goals.

All it takes is a little knowledge about substitutions that may be made to change high-calorie dishes into low-calorie foods with a little variation and lots of thought. Adopt low-calorie vegan dishes into your regular diet and realize that you may enjoy delectable cuisine while maintaining your vegetarian lifestyle.

CHAPTER 7: VEGETARIAN AND NON-VEGETARIAN

Given that the eating habits are unique and evident, the distinction between vegetarianism and non-vegetarianism is well acknowledged

The distinction between vegetarianism and veganism is erroneously made, and there is another branch of the food-eating community that is popularly known as vegan. Although there are no obvious differences between vegan and vegetarian eating styles, many still struggle to classify these food eating groups.

You won't be able to distinguish between vegetarian and vegan diets as a layperson. Because of their evident and obvious similarities, people view these as belonging to the same food consumption groups.

People tend to believe what they see, therefore it's common to observe a vegetarian consuming fresh green salads and a few broccolini for each of their three meals. In actuality, not all vegetarians and vegans consume food in the same way and their practices are not necessarily complementary. Things will become evident after you are aware of this faction's feeding habits. Lacto-ovo-vegetarians are people who eat dairy products, eggs, fruits, and vegetables. One of the most popular and common types of lacto-vegetarian diet is this one. These groups occasionally consume both fish and goods made from chicken. Below are some examples:

Lacto-vegetarians consume dairy products, cereals, fruits, vegetables, and healthy nuts in their diet. The only distinction is that this group doesn't eat eggs.

Vegans: By observing their eating patterns, we can distinguish between vegans and vegetarians. Vegans refrain from consuming dairy products, eggs, or any other kind of animal products in their daily diet. These vegans have abstained from wearing or sporting anything made from animal products.

Follow a diet group for a variety of reasons, including macrobiotics.

Macrobiotic diet refers to a way of eating based on philosophy and spirituality. Before choosing this diet, health-related considerations are also taken into consideration. Foods are divided into negative and positive categories in this diet. Yang is the negative group, and Ying is the positive group. This diet has many progression stages. At all levels, the use of animal products is promoted. The strictest level restricts consumption to only brown rice and bans even fruits and vegetables.

A typical person will undoubtedly mix up the vegetarian and lacto-vegetarian diets. However, adopting a vegan or vegetarian lifestyle is really simple. The benefits and drawbacks of a diet regimen become clear only once you begin to adhere to it. As long as it's healthy and keeps you strong, you ought to embrace all dietary ideologies and eating practices.

Printed in Great Britain
by Amazon